**DAY 1**

Why did the Christ[mas tree go to] school?
— To get a little brighter!

What do elves learn in first grade?
— The elf-abet!

Why was Santa sitting on the clock?
— He wanted to be on time for Christmas!

What do you call a snowman with a big smile?
— Frosty the Grin-man!

  # DAY 1

Why did the reindeer bring a pencil?
— In case it needed to draw the sleigh!

What snack does Santa love in 2025?
— Cool-cookies (they're trending!)

Why don't snowmen like gymnastics?
— They always flip out!

What do you call a Christmas dinosaur?
— A Holly-Rex!

  # DAY 1

What's an elf's favorite sport?
— Snow-ball!

Why did Santa upgrade his phone in 2025?
— For elf-ies in high quality!

How does a snowman travel?
— By icicle-cycle!

What do gingerbread kids sleep on?
— Cookie sheets!

  # DAY 2

Why did Rudolph get good grades?
— He was bright in every subject!

What music do Christmas trees love?
— Wrap music!

Why was the Christmas cookie sad?
— It felt crumby!

What do elves use to clean snow?
— Frost-wipers!

  **DAY 2**

What do you call Santa's dog?
— Santa Paws!

Why did the bell ring so loudly?
— It wanted to jingle all the way!

What do snowmen call their babies?
— Chill-dren!

Why did the elf sit on the computer?
— To keep an eye on the mouse!

  **DAY 2**

Why did Santa wear sneakers?
— He wanted to go sleigh-running!

What do you get when Santa sneezes?
— Cold-flakes!

What do reindeer put on their pizza?
— Moooozzarella!

Why was the present good at math?
— It had great wrapping skills!

  # DAY 3

Why do elves love jokes?
— Because they're elf-laughing all day!

What do snowmen eat for breakfast?
— Frosted flakes!

Why didn't the Christmas tree talk?
— It was too shy to "branch" out!

What's Santa's favorite tea?
— Holly-day tea!

  **DAY 3**

Why did the ornament go to the doctor?
— It felt a little shattered!

What's a snowman's favorite game?
— Freeze tag!

What do elves call their backpacks?
— Jingle packs!

Why did Santa join a dance class?
— He wanted to learn the Snow-Shuffle!

  **DAY 3**

Why was the candy cane hired?
— It was really sweet!

What kind of fish celebrates Christmas?
— A holly-day tuna!

Why did the sleigh break?
— Too many elf-bumps!

What did Santa say to the tired reindeer?
— "You need a nap-deer!"

  # DAY 4

What's a snowman's favorite subject?
— Snow-cial studies!

Why did the cookie stay home?
— It was feeling crumbly!

What do reindeer use to take notes?
— Deer-pencils!

Why did Santa buy a new hat in 2025?
— His old one didn't have enough ho-ho-style!

  **DAY 4**

Why did the elf jump into the snow?
— He wanted to make elf-angels!

What do snowmen wear on their heads?
— Ice caps!

Where do Santa's reindeer get their weather?
— The snow forecast!

Why did Santa go to music school?
— To improve his wrap skills!

  # DAY 4

What do elves use to take selfies?
— Elf-phones!

What do you call Santa when he takes a nap?
— Santa Pause!

Why did the Christmas tree go to the dentist?
— It needed a root canal!

Why don't snowmen like carrots?
— Because they always get stuck on their faces!

  # DAY 5

What does Santa use to fix his suit?
— Santa Tape!

Why was the gingerbread man late?
— He got crumb-led in traffic!

What kind of ball doesn't bounce?
— A snowball!

What's a snowman's favorite snack?
— Ice Krispies!

  **DAY 5**

Why did the reindeer visit the library?
— It wanted to read snow-stories!

What do elves eat on toast?
— Jingle jam!

Why did Santa go to space?
— To see the star on top of the galaxy's tree!

What's Santa's favorite school subject?
— Snow-cial studies!

  **DAY 5** 🎄

What kind of music do elves like?
— Wrap music!

What do you call a reindeer who tells jokes?
— Pun-dolph!

Why do snowmen always smile?
— Because they're chill!

What's Santa's favorite candy?
— Jolly Ranchers!

  **DAY 6**

What do you call a snowman party?
— A snowball!

Why did Santa visit the doctor?
— He had tinsel-itis!

Where do elves keep their money?
— In the snow-bank!

Why did the Christmas lights go to the principal?
— They weren't very bright!

  # DAY 6

What do snowmen take when they get sick?
— Cold medicine!

What's Santa's favorite sport?
— North Pole-vaulting!

Why did the reindeer cross the road?
— To get to Santa's sleigh shop!

What do you call an elf that sings?
— A wrapper!

  **DAY 6**

What do snowmen wear to school?
— Snow-shoes!

Why do elves giggle all the time?
— They have silly-claus!

What's Santa's favorite computer key?
— Ho-Ho-Home!

Why was the snowman staring at the carrots?
— He was picking his nose!

  # DAY 7

What kind of photos do elves love?
— Elfies!

Why did the Christmas tree get in trouble?
— It kept branching out!

What do you call Santa when he loses his pants?
— Saint Knicker-less!

What do you call a snowman with a dog?
— Frosty the Bow-wow!

  **DAY 7**

Why don't reindeer like fast food?
— They can't catch it!

What do you call a snowman with a cold?
— A chilly snowman!

Where does Santa stay on vacation?
— Ho-Ho-Hotel!

Why did the sleigh go to school?
— It wanted to be smarter!

  # DAY 7

Why did Rudolph bring an umbrella?
— Because of rain-deer!

What do snowmen call their pets?
— Flurry friends!

What's Santa's favorite candy bar?
— Snow-Kat!

Why did the ornament break up?
— It couldn't hang anymore!

  # DAY 8

Why do reindeer love telling jokes?
— They love making sleigh-bells ring with laughter!

What's a snowman's favorite dance?
— The Flurry-Freeze!

Why did Santa bring a ladder?
— To reach the star on the tree!

What's the best breakfast for elves?
— Frosted Cheerios!

  # DAY 8

What do elves learn in school?
— Snow-ology!

Why did the cookie visit the doctor?
— It felt crumbly!

What did one snowflake say to another?
— "You're snow cute!"

Why was Santa's belt arrested?
— It was holding up pants!

  **DAY 8**

What do you get when a snowman eats cookies?
— Frosty crumbs!

Why did the reindeer get glasses?
— It had bad "elf" vision!

What do you call Santa's helpers in 2025?
— Elf Influencers!

What do snowpeople take in math?
— Cool-culus!

  # DAY 9

What do snowmen call their big brothers?
— Bro-snow!

Why did the ornament go to school?
— To get a little brighter!

What do you call Santa's cat?
— Santa Claws!

What do gingerbread men use to make phone calls?
— Cookie-phones!

  # DAY 9

Why did the snowman bring a broom?
— To sweep up snowflakes!

Why was Santa so good at karate?
— He had a black-belt in gift wrapping!

What do you call a snowman on roller skates?
— Snow fast!

Why was the elf so good at school?
— He was smartie-claus!

  # DAY 9

What do reindeer use on their noses?
— Snow-lotion!

Why was the snowman proud?
— Because he was cool!

What do Christmas trees wear to parties?
— Tree-tuxedos!

Why did Santa take art class?
— To learn how to draw the sleigh!

 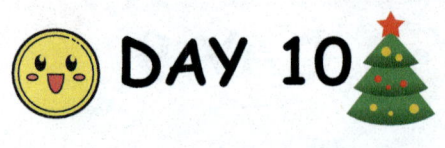 

Why did the gingerbread man buy a coat?
— He felt crumby and cold!

What does Santa use to tell time?
— A North Pole clock!

Why did Rudolph visit the music shop?
— He wanted to learn the jingle bells!

How does Santa clean his suit?
— With snow-suds!

# DAY 10

Why do Christmas lights love school?
— Because they get to be bright!

What kind of key opens Christmas?
— A tur-key!

What's Santa's favorite shape?
— A star!

Why did the kid put his bed in the fireplace?
— He wanted to sleep with Santa!

 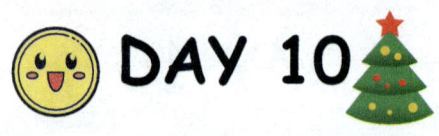 

# DAY 10

Why do snowmen wear hats?
— To stay cool and stylish!

What does Santa say when he's surprised?
— Oh snow you didn't!

Why do elves love puzzles?
— They love to piece things together!

What do snowmen ride?
— Ice cycles!

# DAY 11

Why did the snowman go to the carnival?
— To ride the Frosty-Coaster!

What do you call Santa's little rabbits?
— Bunny Claus!

What do reindeer say before telling a joke?
— "This will sleigh you!"

What do elves drink in the morning?
— Jingle juice!

 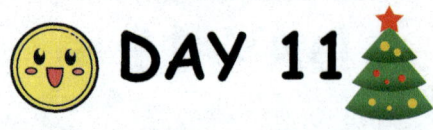 

# DAY 11

What kind of math do snowmen do?
— Ice-ometry!

What does Santa use for hair styling?
— Sleigh spray!

Why did the Christmas tree blush?
— It saw the presents opened!

Where do snowmen keep their money?
— In a snowbank!

# DAY 11

What do Santa's cows say?
— Moo-mas!

Why did Rudolph bring a broom?
— To sweep up snow prints!

Why did the elf eat candy canes?
— He needed a minty boost!

Where do reindeer go after Christmas?
— On deer-cation!

 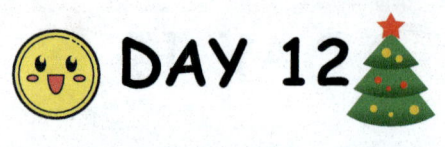 

# DAY 12

> Why did the snowman go to the doctor?
> — He felt a bit frosty!

> Why don't Santa's helpers fight?
> — They have elf-control!

> Why do elves love trees?
> — They're full of ornament opportunities!

> What does Santa read every night?
> — Snow-time stories!

# DAY 12

What is Rudolph's favorite weather?
— Snow and shine!

Why did the snowman call the police?
— Someone stole his nose!

What do reindeer say on birthdays?
— Hap-deer Birthday!

What do you call Santa's helpers in the kitchen?
— Baking elves!

# DAY 12

What dance do snowmen love?
— The Flurry-Freeze!

Why did Santa's suit shrink?
— He washed it in hot cocoa!

What do elves use to cut wrapping paper?
— Elf-scissors!

What's a gingerbread man's favorite sport?
— Cookie kick!

# DAY 13

Why did Santa go to school?
— To improve his Ho-Ho-homework!

What do you get when you cross a reindeer with snow?
— A Frosty deer!

Why did the snowman read a book?
— To chill and learn!

What game do elves like best?
— Elf and Seek!

Where do snowmen dance?
— At the snowball!

What do you call Santa with no beard?
— Santa Who?

What's a snowman's favorite drink?
— Ice tea!

Why did the tree go to bed?
— It was tired of standing!

# DAY 13

Why did the reindeer bring soap?
— To take a snow bath!

What do elves ride to school?
— Jingle buses!

What do snowmen wear in summer?
— Puddles!

Why was the gingerbread man confused?
— He got crumb-fused!

 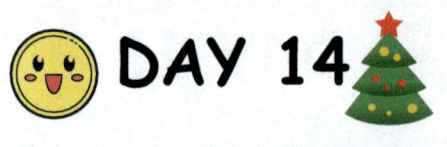 

# DAY 14

Why did Santa start gardening?
— He loves Ho-Ho-Hoses!

What do reindeer use on their hooves?
— Mistle-toe polish!

Why did the snowman bring a ladder?
— To reach the coolest clouds!

What do you call a dancing elf?
— Twinkle Toes!

Why do snowmen love surprises?
— They freeze with excitement!

Why did Santa eat at the computer?
— He wanted cookies and clicks!

How do elves travel?
— By sleigh bus!

What kind of boots does Santa wear?
— Snow-boots!

 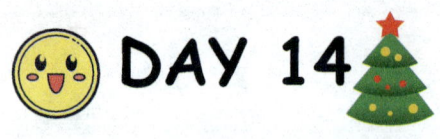 

# DAY 14

What do you get when Santa sneezes?
— Cold-y presents!

Why did Rudolph go to art class?
— He loved draw-deer-ing!

What's a snowman's favorite treat?
— Ice cream cake!

Why was the ornament so quiet?
— It didn't want to crack up!

Why do Christmas trees knit?
— They love needlework!

What do snowmen take for headaches?
— Ice-pirin!

What do you call Santa's laundry?
— Claus and effect!

Why did the reindeer stay cold?
— It forgot its warm antlers!

 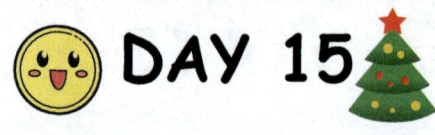 

Why did Santa's helper take notes?
— To become elf-ucated!

What do snowmen eat at lunch?
— Chill-dogs!

Why don't snowballs ever get mad?
— They just let it slide!

What's Santa's favorite keyboard key?
— Ho-Ho-Home!

# DAY 15

Where do elves store cookies?
— In jingle jars!

What do you call a snowman in July?
— A puddle!

Why did Santa go to the gym?
— To work on his jingle muscles!

Why did the tree start singing?
— It wanted to be on Star Top Idol!

# DAY 16

Why did Rudolph love school?
— He was bright and sharp!

What do snowmen eat for dessert?
— Icy pie!

Why did Santa paint his sleigh blue?
— He wanted it to be cool!

What kind of puppy does Santa have?
— A Fur-ling!

Why did the bell go to bed?
— It was tired of ringing!

Why don't elves like tests?
— They prefer present-ations!

What do snowmen call their moms?
— Iced Mommy!

What do Santa's helpers learn in science?
— Snow-biology!

 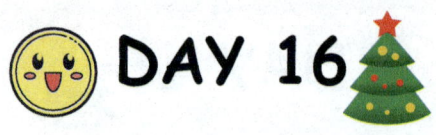 

# DAY 16

Why did the snowman skip dessert?
— He was stuffed with snow!

Why was the elf good at spelling?
— He knew the elf-abet!

What's Santa's favorite ride?
— The Jolly-Coaster!

What did the reindeer wear to the party?
— Snow-glasses!

# DAY 17

Where do snowmen keep their money?
— In snow-wallets!

Why did the elf take a nap?
— He was exhausted from laughing!

What's a snowman's favorite pet?
— A snow-pup!

Why did Santa wear sunglasses?
— His future was too bright!

 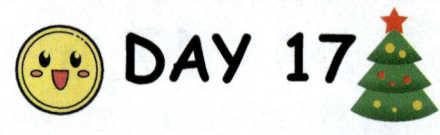 

# DAY 17

What kind of cereal do elves eat?
— Jingle O's!

Why did the snowman go to school?
— To learn snow-ledge!

What do reindeer use to clean their sleigh?
— Sleigh-sponge!

What's Santa's favorite snack?
— Ho-Ho-Hos!

# DAY 17

What do you call a fast snowman?
— Snow Zoom!

Why did Rudolph cross the road?
— Because it was the snow-way!

Why did Santa write a book?
— He had great "Claus" for ideas!

What did Frosty do at the beach?
— Melt and relax!

 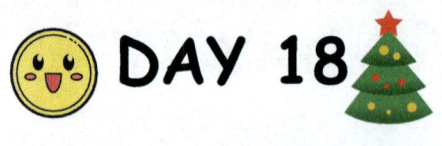 

# DAY 18

Why did the elf sit on the pencil?
— To draw elf-ies!

What do snowmen take on vacations?
— Snow-suitcases!

Why did Santa love video games in 2025?
— He loved sleigh racing!

What do you get when a snowball tells a joke?
— Ice-laughter!

# DAY 18

**What did the reindeer say to Santa?**
— I'm "snow" excited!

**Why was the cookie so cool?**
— Because it had chill chips!

**How does Santa swim?**
— In the North Pool!

**What do snowmen read?**
— Cool-stories!

 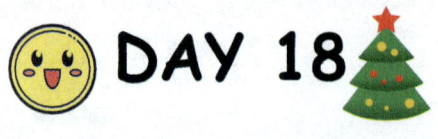 

# DAY 18

Why was the elf so smart?
— He had elf-brains!

What's a reindeer's favorite type of math?
— Snow-division!

What does Santa do after Christmas?
— Chill out!

Where do elves go for fun?
— Jingle Park!

Why did the snowman need a tissue?
— He had snow sniffles!

What kind of joke is a snowman?
— A corny one!

What's Santa's favorite snack in 2025?
— Peppermint popcorn!

Why do reindeer make great friends?
— They're always deer to you!

# DAY 19

Why did the elf wear glasses?
— He lost elf-control!

What do snowmen call their hats?
— Cool caps!

Why did Santa bring string to his workshop?
— To tie up loose ends!

What do snowmen do in summer?
— Melt-fun vacation!

# DAY 19

Why did Santa jump in the snow?
— To make Santa angels!

What does a snowman take in school?
— Chill-dren's math!

What do gingerbread men use to text?
— Cookie-phones!

What's Santa's favorite movie?
— Frozen gifts!

 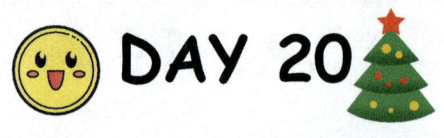 

# DAY 20

Why did the snowman bring his backpack?
— He was going to Snow School!

Why did the reindeer love music?
— He had horns!

What kind of car does Santa drive?
— A Toy-ota!

What do elves wear in rainy weather?
— Snow boots!

# DAY 20

Why did the tree bring scissors?
— To trim itself!

Why do snowmen love Saturdays?
— They get to chillax!

What's Santa's favorite sandwich?
— Merry Cheese!

Why was Rudolph always smiling?
— He was merry and bright!

 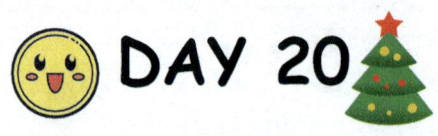 

# DAY 20

Why did the snowman become a teacher?
— He had snowledge to share!

What do elves bake for fun?
— Jingle Pies!

Why did Santa learn karate?
— To kick off Christmas!

What does the snow say to kids?
— Snow much fun!

Why did the elf go on stage?
— To show his elf-talent!

Why was the ornament so happy?
— It was well hung!

What do elves write on?
— North Pole notebooks!

Why did the snowman go to the party?
— He was a cool guy!

 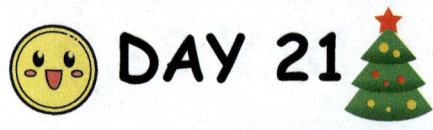 

# DAY 21

What do reindeer use to style hair?
— Sleigh-gel!

Why did Santa wear a helmet?
— Slippery sleigh rides!

Why was the gift good at school?
— It was well-wrapped!

How does Santa greet kids?
— Ho-Ho-Hello!

# DAY 21

What do snowmen call their kids?
— Chill-dren!

Why do reindeer wear bells?
— Because their horns don't ring!

What do Christmas trees wear?
— Tree-mendous sweaters!

What did the snowman say to the sun?
— Don't make me puddle!

 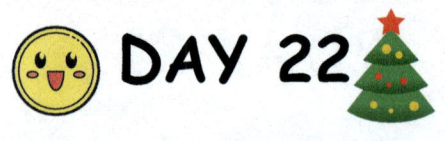 

# DAY 22

What do elves use to clean?
— Jingle mops!

Why did the reindeer yell "Woohoo"?
— He heard bells ring!

Where do snowmen meet?
— At the cool club!

What's Santa's favorite fruit?
— Merry Berries!

# DAY 22

Why did the gingerbread man join school?
— To get cookie-smart!

What do you call Santa when he's tired?
— Sleepy Claus!

Why don't snowmen argue?
— They keep things cool!

What do you call an elf who is funny?
— A Laughing Helper!

 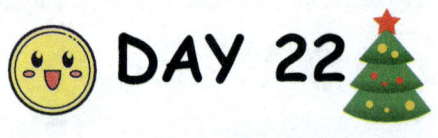 

# DAY 22

Why do bells love school?
— They get to ring answers!

Why did Santa go to the beach?
— For Sandy Claus time!

What do snowmen eat with lunch?
— Snow-fry!

What do elves put in their lunch?
— Jolly jelly!

# DAY 23

Why did the snowman blush?
— He saw the snow blower!

What did Santa say to the elves?
— Snow-body works harder than you!

What do polar bears say for Christmas?
— Fur-ry Christmas!

Why did the reindeer get homework?
— He was snow special!

 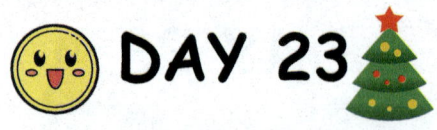 

# DAY 23

Where do elves store money?
— Snow-wallets!

Why did the snowman go to bed early?
— He was melted out!

What do reindeer use to brush teeth?
— Snow paste!

Why did Santa bring a camera?
— To take elfies!

# DAY 23

**Why did the gingerbread man laugh?**
— He had sweet jokes!

**What do elves listen to?**
— Jingle tunes!

**Why did Santa's sleigh stop?**
— It was out of snow-gas!

**Why did the snowman wear sunglasses?**
— Because he was so cool!

 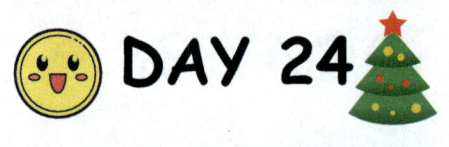 

# DAY 24

What do snowmen order at fast food?
— Icy burgers!

What do reindeer sing?
— Fawn in a Manger!

Why did the present go to class?
— It wanted to be gifted!

How does Santa stay organized?
— He makes a list—snow kidding!

# DAY 24

Why did the snowman eat snowflakes?
— They tasted flake-tastic!

What do you call Santa's secret agent?
— Double Ho-Ho-Ho!

What do elves wear to bed?
— Snow-jamas!

What's Santa's favorite fish?
— Jollyfish!

 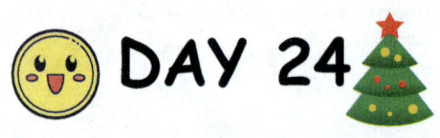 

Why don't snowballs ever get lost?
— They always roll home!

What do reindeer call their grannies?
— Granny deer!

Why did Santa wear boots?
— To stay snow-proof!

Why did the gingerbread man smile?
— Just for cookie-joy!

# DAY 25

Why did Rudolph write a diary?
— He had sleigh-worthy stories!

What do snowmen like on crackers?
— Snow butter!

Why do elves carry rulers?
— To measure Santa's joy!

What's Santa's favorite pizza?
— Snow-lice Pizza!

Why did the snowman stay calm?
— He kept his cool!

How do elves send messages?
— Jingle mail!

Why did Rudolph visit the computer?
— To check his reindeer mail!

What do snowmen do in free time?
— Chill out!

What kind of bird gives Christmas presents?
— Robo-Robin!

Why don't Christmas trees knit fast?
— Too many needles!

Why did Santa call tech support?
— His elf-phone froze!

What do snowmen do before bed?
— Put on their snow-jamas!

Printed in Dunstable, United Kingdom